NLP

Highly Effective Instruments For Restructuring
Behavioral Patterns And Optimizing Personal Capacities

*(Harnessing The Potential Of Human Communication With
The Aid Of Machine Intelligence)*

Dominic Wheeler

TABLE OF CONTENT

Fundamental Principles Of Natural Language Processing 1

What is NLP? 1

Developing Proficiency In Neuro-Linguistic Programming 26

Conceptual Diagrams And Sorting Systems 36

Natural Language Processing And The Management Of Weight Loss 58

The Fundamental Assumptions Of Neuro Linguistic Programming 65

Official Neuro-Linguistic Guide 79

Enhancing Vocal And Physical Confidence: A Comprehensive Guide 109

Conduct Calibration Solely Based On Behavior 120

Dissociation: Detach Yourself From Adverse Encounters 130

Nlp Techniques: Rapport 141

Fundamental Principles Of Natural Language Processing

What is NLP?

Neurolinguistic Programming (NLP) offers a comprehensive framework for understanding and analyzing human behavior within the realm of communication. It imparts knowledge on the processes employed to generate various emotions such as joy, sadness, euphoria, or anger within us, elucidating the strategies we employ to prompt specific actions and ultimately secure desired outcomes.

It serves as a model rather than a theory, thus its purpose is to simulate effective practices rather than formulating theories or establishing links with psychological or philosophical systems or approaches.

One reason for this is that by understanding the techniques that successful individuals employ instinctively, we can deliberately adopt and implement these strategies to attain success in various professional or emotional aspects.

Natural Language Processing encompasses a wide range of techniques and competencies that enable the cultivation of exemplary states for effective communication, ultimately resulting in transformative outcomes. Over the course of the subsequent pages, we shall examine its influence on individuals as well as its application to others.

Fundamental tenets of natural language processing in regards to human nature

Initially, researchers in the field of NLP conducted studies on skilled therapists. Fritz Perls, an early subject of study, pioneered the field of Gestalt therapy, which emphasized the importance of present-moment awareness. He possessed a remarkable ability to discern nonverbal cues and swiftly gather insights from interpersonal interactions.

He devoted his attention to the antithesis of psychoanalysis, which necessitated extensive dedication and rigorous introspection in order to comprehend the intricate process of personal development.

Virginia Satir was the second therapist examined, renowned for her contributions to the development of family therapy within her field. She did not demonstrate a commitment to solely working with the troublesome family member, but rather focused on addressing the needs and dynamics of the entire familial unit.

He expressed that every behavior and action constituted an integral element of the familial dynamic. He ascertained that by exclusively focusing on an individual, the familial framework would recurrently lead him back to the same predicament, thus underscoring the imperative nature of engaging with the entire family unit.

The NLP pioneers also examined Milton Erickson, a highly skilled physician renowned for his development of clinical hypnotherapy. Unlike Perls and Satir, Erickson took a distinctively unique approach, demonstrating exceptional ingenuity in obtaining seemingly miraculous outcomes.

Another individual of note was Moshe Feldenkrais, a gentleman tasked with facilitating bodily recovery and restoration through his remarkable manual healing techniques.

The fundamental operational principles of NLP, denoted as "presuppositions," reveal the core, unifying convictions held by these four notable individuals who were closely examined in order to identify the most efficacious approaches, thus culminating in the establishment of the cornerstones upon which NLP is built.

Consensus was reached among all these experts regarding the core tenets concerning human nature. We will outline two of the utmost significant tenets. The initial option is as follows:

There exists no internal adversary.

There exists no malevolent entity residing within you, working in opposition to your desires. One can remove those convictions which cause an individual to perceive themselves as damaged or pitted against their own inner being. Individuals engage in self-harming behaviors, such as excessive alcohol consumption or perpetrating acts of violence, driven by their perception of necessity.

Certain actions may appear irrational to the majority, however, it is imperative to comprehend an individual's perspective and thought processes, as they serve as the impetus for their behavior.

The second conviction is:

Behind every action lies a underlying positive motive.

Consider for a moment a scenario that directly pertains to your personal experience: when you encounter an individual, you may observe involuntary trembling of your legs and a noticeable quiver in your voice. What is the underlying cause of these physical reactions? There is no inherent fault within you; rather, your mind signals that encountering this individual may lead to negative consequences, prompting self-preservation and cautionary measures to avoid confrontation.

Through the use of NLP, it becomes feasible to observe the cognitive processes and discern the underlying pattern that gives rise to a specific reaction. Subsequently, efforts can be exerted to modify said pattern.

Please bear in mind that there is no internal antagonist that acts in opposition to you, and that every action is propelled by a positive motive. Your cognitive processes currently function to the best of their abilities, yet they may require modifications given that the majority of individuals undergo programming between the ages of 2 and 5. Unless we alter the software implemented during that period, we will persistently replicate behavioral patterns on autopilot, often unconsciously.

What is the efficacy of NLP in application?

There exist various justifications for undertaking the study of NLP, primarily to gain an understanding of fundamental aspects of human cognition and self-perception. Our objective is to implement these skill sets in practical settings where they can yield substantial outcomes.

NLP plays a crucial role in the present day. We reside in a perpetually evolving technological realm, wherein our constant connectivity enables us to engage regularly with colleagues, loved ones, and individuals of significance. We are often preoccupied with responding to inquiries, leaving little room for deep contemplation.

In the subsequent sections, you will unravel cognitive patterns and acquire the skills to effectively regulate them, not only for personal advancement but also for effective leadership of others.

You will acquire a novel approach to interpersonal interactions, gaining insight into others' perspectives and emotions.

Gaining knowledge about the functioning of our cognitive processes

Despite our shared neurological structure and learning processes, as well as potential overlaps in our concerns, it is important to acknowledge that our thoughts and perspectives are not universally identical. Each individual possesses their own distinctive thought process, thereby rendering us distinctively unique, akin to the distinctiveness of our fingerprints.

Unbeknownst to us, we inadvertently acclimate ourselves to minor irritations and constraints on our emotional and mental capacities throughout our existence. It is imperative that every individual ascertain and safeguard boundaries, as this is instrumental in cultivating a sense of personal safety and fostering acknowledgment and adherence to our preferences by others.

Engaging in activities like delivering public speeches, cultivating positive habits, assuming greater responsibility in certain matters - all present opportunities for personal growth beyond our current capabilities. However, it is disheartening to witness many individuals relinquishing their efforts prematurely, citing the adage that "old parrots cannot learn to speak." Nonetheless, this notion is far from accurate.

It necessitates the utilization of appropriate tools. Through the identification of cognitive processes, one can effectively implement the necessary modifications. The most effective approach to bringing about transformation entails comprehending the mechanism of emotions' formation and endeavoring to modify them.

What is the process by which our emotions are generated?

They are inherently exposed to various stimuli, such as the sensory experience upon awakening, encompassing the functioning of the coffee maker and the aroma of brewing coffee, the sound of a weeping child, a barking dog necessitating a walk, the latest news on a preferred website, or the presence of a playing television. All of these occurrences are neural stimulations that transpire within the confines of your cerebral cortex.

Upon the receipt of this information, it is promptly analyzed, whereby you attribute to it a significance imbued with emotional connotations. You gave this feeling. One might perceive it as a positive occurrence, where the joyful dog greets your presence, the coffee maker emits a melodious sound, and a child's cry is swiftly transformed into silence through affection. Alternatively, one may experience displeasure due to the persistent barking of the noisy dog and the relentless noise made by the child. Weeping while the coffee maker lacks any supply of coffee.

Both of the aforementioned scenarios serve as stimuli, encapsulating meaningful and emotional content that consequently elicits specific responses. Through gaining an insightful understanding of emotional responses and the significance you ascribe to your thoughts, it becomes feasible to revisit those thoughts and actively endeavor to modify them. One possible alternative way to express this idea in a formal tone could be: "For instance, it is advisable to meticulously document one's thoughts and subsequently deliberate on more optimal responses."

The concern at hand pertains to the frequent occurrence of solely perceiving the initial stimulus, while the interpretation of the emotion connected to said stimulus remains beyond our conscious awareness. Attempt to articulate ideas in the following manner:

I experience a sense of well-being in your presence."

"You made me angry".

The conduct of that particular client significantly affected my overall experience today."

Irrespective of the manner in which these expressions are articulated, the true source of my emotions does NOT stem from the individual in question. We consistently assume the role of ascribing significance to every situation we encounter. Our emotional state is not influenced by other individuals or the surrounding environment, as there is no discernible causal relationship. This can be evidenced by the fact that disparate emotional reactions arise amongst individuals when faced with identical circumstances.

From this perspective, it is impossible for anyone to elicit a specific emotion within us. The sequence of events entails an individual carrying out an action, whereby I, within my internal thought process, make a deliberate choice to correlate a specific emotion with said action. Ultimately, it is incumbent upon us to bear the responsibility for our emotional well-being consistently, independent of external circumstances.

The realms residing in our cognitive faculties

Perhaps you possess an understanding of what is genuine and what is not. Consider the following scenario: You possess a twin brother with whom you both cohabit within the confines of a shared living space. While one might assume that the reality experienced by your brother aligns with your own, let me clarify that this assumption is unfounded.

From the moment of our birth, we become aware of our surroundings. Initially, there is an overwhelming sense of disorder as the mind struggles to comprehend the flood of incomprehensible information: countless images, sounds, scents, tastes, and bodily sensations. The mind initiates the process of arranging and categorizing various elements, utilizing various forms of communication such as language. Its cognitive functioning largely relies on the utilization of sensory inputs such as visual images, auditory stimuli, gustatory experiences, tactile sensations, and olfactory perceptions. They are fundamental elements in the realm of consciousness.

The perception and experience of the world around you are essentially products of your own cognitive processes, exclusive to your individual consciousness. The cognitions of your mind shape the reality you experience, the interpersonal connections you cultivate, your behavioral patterns in social contexts, your self-perceptions, and the perceptual frameworks you construct.

Your brain is equipped with the faculties of sight, hearing, sensations, taste, and smell, yet it does not employ them to an equal degree. In due course, you will attain a more comprehensive understanding of the subject matter I am discussing.

What is the nature of your introspective experience?

Observe the attire you are adorned in, along with the methodical manner in which you have donned them and extracted them from the wardrobe. In summary, the entire procedure culminated in its eventual implementation. Now consider the garments you wore yesterday, utilizing this method enables you to retrieve that information and reengage with the sensations you experienced during that time. The mental faculty constructed that visual representation for you.

It is important to bear in mind that one's perception of an image may not correspond identically to that of the previous day, as it is influenced by the emotional experiences encountered in each unique situation. It is imperative to have a door installed at the entrance of the residence. Upon perusing this information, it is likely that you have contemplated the presence of your own door. As a resident of that area, you are undoubtedly aware of the door in question. I urge you to vividly envision its characteristics and intricacies. Having considered the matter, please proceed to uncover the item, as it will emit a distinct sound upon being unsealed. Experience the strength you apply when you access it, be it delicate like a gentle breeze or substantial as it makes contact with the ground.

Carefully consider all aspects of this matter, including each individual sensation and the information that has been stored in your memory instinctively. You will observe that you possess a significant amount of stored information.

Now envision the majestic peaks of the mountains, amidst a wide expanse of lush greenery. Picture yourself reclining on this verdant landscape, feeling the softness of the grass beneath you, with your elbow gently making contact with the dampened earth. For individuals who are right-handed, envision the scenario where it is the left elbow in question, and conversely, for those who are left-handed, imagine it to be the right elbow. Now endeavor to utilize the elbow with lesser dexterity to attempt scratching an object. Please endeavor to form the initial letter of your name by employing your imaginative faculties. Whilst perusing this text, you undoubtedly may have observed the letter imprinted upon the Earth's surface, and surely you must have noticed the blemished grass resulting from your own agency. Prior to initiating any of these actions, the lyrics were initially visualized within your mind.

What is your perception of that correspondence? Certain individuals may perceive it through written text, while others might encounter it through conspicuous neon signage, large-scale billboards, or the use of ornate gothic typography. Your cognition perceived all of these details, including the ability to delineate writing methods using your non-dominant elbow.

Consider alternative options, contemplate the shoreline, envision familiar locations encountered in your daily routine, the aromas linked with the act of opening doors, and the auditory experiences upon entering your residence or workplace. When considering each of these scenarios, various emotions are experienced, such as the anxiety invoked by the odor emanating from the door adjacent to the dentist's office, or the pleasant fragrance encountered upon entering the room that houses a beloved individual. , from which you derive delight and joy. Each location evokes various sentiments, encompassing both positive and negative impressions, often appearing neutral on certain occasions. They encompass a plethora of sensations that encompass your cognitive faculties with a wealth of information.

The brain possesses the capacity to categorize and store all of this information. It encompasses the entirety of your cognitive, perceptual, emotional, auditory, and imaginative experiences.

The influential force of anchors

Anchors serve as the vessels of our collective memories and possess the potential for both positive and negative transformation. They possess significant authority, as they grant us the ability to tap into that potency or vulnerability. This is the point at which all the senses examined in the preceding section come into play.

Anchors are employed by each one of us on a daily basis. It is an affiliation that arises through specific cogitations, perceptions, conditions, and stimuli. The process of establishing anchors, whether in oneself or in others, is comprised of two stages. Initially, the individual is placed in the desired state of being anchored, wherein they are then subjected to a distinct stimulus. An alternative approach entails prompting him to recollect a particular instance in which he experienced a desired emotional or sensory state. During this recollection, the individual actively engages all their senses. Subsequently, repetitive exposure to a specific stimulus, such as the application of pressure on an arm, would be implemented.

Reflect upon a specific instance in your life, characterized by a resolute and confident mindset. Immerse yourself within that particular scenario, fully engaging with its circumstances. Recall that particular experience, and when you recollect it fully, apply pressure to a specific area of your body while uttering the phrase "I am capable." Now consider an alternative scenario of similar nature and, upon achieving a superior position, repeat the aforementioned action. Engage in the repetition process approximately seven instances, thereby establishing an ample number of robust mental and emotional anchors within your being. Take a moment to consider the pivotal choice you intend to make, and initiate the anchor signal. That is the level of simplicity that accompanies your approach.

A convenient method for individuals to establish an anchor can be through auditory stimuli. As an illustration, consider the scenario in which you are acting as a trainer and incorporate a tabata workout routine accompanied by specific music. Consequently, all the trainees become attuned to the anchor, recognizing that it signifies the commencement of a particular set of exercises with predetermined intervals of action and rest. That is a rudimentary anchoring device.

Developing Proficiency In Neuro-Linguistic Programming

In order to effectively achieve your objectives, the field of NLP involves the process of reprogramming your cognitive faculties. This technique of achieving success is unfamiliar to many individuals, but numerous motivational speakers are diligently exerting efforts to educate people about its efficacy. Extensive evidence has demonstrated its effectiveness in transforming attitudes, emotions, and beliefs of a considerable number of individuals.

In order to proficiently acquire expertise in the practice of NLP, it is essential to undertake a series of sequential measures, ultimately enabling the attainment of numerous objectives in life. This chapter delineates the aforementioned steps.

A. Gaining a comprehensive understanding of the situation at hand.

Engaging in this particular undertaking is paramount in the attainment of proficiency in NLP, thereby enabling you to effectively actualize your aspirations in life. NLP is a complex approach that poses challenges in comprehension, as a significant number of individuals struggle to regulate their thoughts or articulate themselves even in mundane aspects of their existence.

NLP has the potential to help individuals overcome these two components and reassess their entire being, facilitating the transformation of hindering factors and barriers that have impeded achievements and hindered the realization of personal values, such as success. The process of mastering NLP and transforming one's values and habits is a lifelong journey, and therefore it is imperative not to rush in achieving remarkable outcomes within a limited span of time.

B. Devote a sufficient amount of time to acquiring a deeper understanding of NLP.

Numerous individuals discuss NLP, without possessing a comprehensive understanding of its intricacies. In order to attain significant success with NLP, it is imperative to thoroughly comprehend and master its concepts and techniques. As an illustration, it is noteworthy that an extensive amount of information pertaining to natural language processing can be found within various media sources. A number of these assertions are factual, whereas others are false. Verify your personal perception of reality, exercising due diligence in comprehending its true essence.

Comprehend how NLP operates. In the majority of circumstances in life, we acknowledge the challenges that come our way and promptly endeavor to find a resolution. A prime illustration of this propensity is observed when we opt to alleviate a headache by means of ingesting medication. NLP exhibits notable distinctness as it aptly acknowledges the underlying issues and comprehends that the instigation of said issues stems from the information that has been assimilated into one's cognitive faculties. NLP endeavors to instill in individuals the understanding that they possess the agency to address their difficulties, subsequently equipping them with a range of methodologies to effectively resolve said challenges. If you possess a comprehensive comprehension of the mechanisms at play, incorporating NLP towards the resolution of myriad everyday challenges, in alignment with the accomplishment of your personal aspirations, shall be rendered surprisingly facile.

C. Please be aware that there exist multiple approaches to achieving proficiency in NLP.

NLP exhibits inherent expansiveness analogous to the intricate workings of the human mind, wherein one can discern and explore manifold avenues to achieve desired outcomes with NLP. Natural Language Processing (NLP) is a versatile instrument that can be employed in various aspects of life. To illustrate, there exists a competence for conquering apprehension as well as a proficiency for mitigating unfavorable sentiments. If you are inclined to dedicate your focus towards a constructive aspect of life, specifically physical fitness, there is a proficiency in which you can engage. Natural Language Processing encompasses all the necessary tools and techniques to diligently specify and effectively employ your preferences, leading to streamlining various aspects of your life.

D. Feel free to thoroughly investigate at your own discretion.

There is a wide range of approaches to leveraging NLP techniques for the achievement of your life objectives; engaging in diversified experimentation will ultimately prove highly advantageous to you. To attain favorable outcomes in the realm of NLP, it is advisable to direct your focus inward, delving deeper into your emotions and thoughts.

It is advisable to scrutinize your intrinsic values and examine your perception of the world and its workings. Anticipate uncovering a plethora of information that may be previously unknown to you, which may evoke a sense of unease. Nevertheless, it is imperative to achieve NLP expertise by undertaking this task.

E. Interpret phenomena according to your own perspective.

During your exploration of self-discovery through the practice of NLP, you will uncover numerous revelations. Given the absence of external guidance in this skill, it will be incumbent upon you to ascertain your comprehension of matters and discern your personal life objectives. Once you have achieved mastery in utilizing NLP to pinpoint your constraining elements, this outcome will follow suit.

F. Do not confine yourself.

Truly, there are no boundaries to what the human mind is capable of achieving.

Hence, it is imperative that you refrain from imposing limitations upon yourself. What is the rationale behind the inclination to impose limitations upon oneself, considering the vast potential for achievement that can be harnessed through the power of one's intellect? Once NLP is employed for swift resolution, there would be no necessity to address your phobias any further. To achieve a more prosperous future, establish ambitious goals and strive to push your boundaries to accomplish as much as possible.

G. Enjoy it

If you lack enthusiasm for altering your belief patterns, your proficiency in NLP will be limited, underscoring the significance of finding enjoyment in the process. Ultimately, incorporating enjoyment into your efforts to overcome addictions, fears, obsessions, and other hindrances will prove beneficial in yielding more favorable outcomes.

To overcome these constraining factors, there are numerous strategies at your disposal, enabling you to promptly restore order to your life. Please be aware that in the presence of such constraining elements, your perception of NLP should align precisely with your current sentiment. Endeavor to distance yourself from following a preconceived trajectory; instead, endeavor to carve out a unique path for yourself. Embrace the opportunity to thoroughly indulge in the pleasures along the way, and bear witness to the astonishing moments that will undoubtedly unfold.

Conceptual Diagrams And Sorting Systems

Mind Map

Every correlation and affiliation that one establishes in their day-to-day existence becomes an integral component of their cognitive framework. In the event that you lack familiarity with the visual representation of neurons within the brain, they manifest as a stellar arrangement resembling a burst of light, or analogously, like an egg that has been delicately fractured upon a stovetop and subsequently exhibits numerous outgrowths. These branches collectively constitute a sophisticated neural network that integrates all the requisite information for the retention and application of your life experiences.

If you engage in automotive transportation, you have likely consulted a comprehensive printed map delineating an extensive geographical area, encompassing the entire nation, and comprised of major thoroughfares, secondary roads, and prominent points of interest. Your cognitive processes depict your voyage in a comparable manner. You will perceive your surroundings not through roads and highways, but rather through your sensory encounters as an integral component of this life atlas.

Mind maps are subjective representations of the external world derived from our sensory perceptions and their influence on our personal encounters with existence. They exhibit discernment, being capable of excluding numerous details to present a concise depiction of your present reality or life domain. The map you create depends on your observations or the alterations you wish to make.

The perception of reality we possess is distinct and individualized. There is no other individual on Earth who possesses an identical map as you.

Filters

Furthermore, aside from possessing an individualized mind map, one also possesses filters. Filters serve to shape the nature of the environment in which we reside; functioning akin to a fine mesh screen through which our conceptions of reality are sieved. Should your criteria be aligned with the tenets of excellence, you will perceive and seek out such qualities in your interactions with the world. Conversely, if your criteria are imbued with a predisposition to identify faults and issues in all things, you will inevitably manifest a propensity to discover such aspects.

If an individual nurtures numerous constraining beliefs as a result of pessimistic cognitive habits, convictions, and perspectives, the ensuing implications will present a dearth in their perception of the world. The world can encompass both beauty and opportunity, contingent upon the filters through which you elect to perceive it.

The choice of language serves as a mechanism of filtration. Each individual will hold a distinct emotional response to a word such as "sunset." The sensory encounter of a sunset varies across the maps of different individuals.

Beliefs are filters, too. One's convictions have a profound effect on their perspective and conduct.

NLP also serves as a filter - a framework that does not necessitate altering one's values or beliefs, but rather encourages an approach to life driven by a willingness to explore and an inquisitive mindset. It serves as a paradigm of distinction, yet does not assert any inherent veracity: your individuality is undeniable and cannot be universally categorized, however, these tools and techniques function as a discerning mechanism, regardless.

Basic NLP Filters

NLP categorizes these filters as frames. NLP encompasses a total of five behavioral frames. They are:

Initial framework prioritizes results over challenges.

This phenomenon can also be referred to as the "attribution framework." Directing attention towards challenges instead of desired results prompts individuals to inquire, "what is the cause of this predicament," as opposed to "what actions can be taken to improve the situation."

The second frame focuses on the manner in which something occurs, rather than delving into the underlying reasons for it.

Inquiring about the "how" rather than the "why" will facilitate comprehension of the problem's underlying framework. Continuously inquiring about the reasons behind matters will not lead to an enhanced understanding of the methodology for resolving the issues at hand.

Third Frame = constructive criticism as opposed to a lack of success

In the field of NLP, it is often stated that there exists no failure, but rather outcomes. Failure is essentially a term employed to characterize an outcome that does not align with one's desired objective, yet it ultimately serves as insightful input towards achieving the preferred outcomes.

Within the fourth frame lies a realm of potential rather than obligatory outcomes.

Observing the feasibility of something has the power to redirect one's attention. Focusing exclusively on an essential requirement restricts opportunities for growth. Each and every one of us possesses basic needs, yet by adhering to a constrained perception of reality, we forfeit the abundance of opportunities that lie within the realm of possibilities.

The fifth frame pertains to cultivating curiosity and fascination, rather than relying on assumptions.

In order to embark upon the acquisition of new knowledge and embracing transformative adjustments, a certain degree of inquisitiveness and engagement is imperative. By solely relying on assumptions, one greatly restricts their perception of reality, thereby depriving themselves of a more logical and enlightened encounter.

The chart outlining the trajectory of your existence forms a vibrant and intricate fresco capturing the myriad encounters of your journey perceived through your faculties. You consistently expand upon this foundation on a daily basis, and by acquiring proficiency in NLP techniques, you provide yourself with novel avenues that lead to the pursuit of excellence.

Circle of Distinction

This exercise possesses immense utility and can be employed for a myriad of objectives. The fundamental concept entails the selection of four exemplary individuals, whose qualities are combined to form a cohesive composite character. It encompasses a few concepts from the field of modeling, as well as the typical ways in which we, as humans, engage with exemplary figures.

Role Models

Humans have a proclivity to imitate conduct that they find appealing in their counterparts. We internalize behaviors observed in the company of our most esteemed peers. During early stages of development, individuals tend to internalize behaviors from their parents and siblings, potentially leading to subsequent challenges if negative behaviors are acquired. In the timeless debate concerning the role of upbringing versus genetics, Fundamentally, nature refers to the totality of acquired knowledge and behavior that is assimilated without deliberate intent, shaped by the environment during the process of nurture. We invariably acquire beliefs, both empowering and constraining, from our parental figures, often without conscious awareness. In the event that one is fortunate to have exceedingly positive parents who consistently demonstrate positive behavior (an exceedingly uncommon occurrence), that individual is bestowed with good fortune. If you are similar to the majority of individuals, you were raised by parents who predominantly engaged in practical learning experiences, thereby unconsciously assimilating certain unfavorable traits. The exercise presented in this chapter exhibits a certain degree of resemblance, or perhaps it can be perceived as such with sufficient dedication and diligence.

General Process

The idea is simple. You establish four exemplary figures. Exemplary individuals who embody distinct qualities that you aspire to acquire. As an illustration, in the context of sports, one might opt for a role model who exemplifies agility, another who embodies stamina, a third who epitomizes strength, and a fourth who embodies unwavering mental resilience. If one were to utilize this for artistic endeavors, it might be prudent to consider selecting an exemplar for each aspect, namely creativity, emotional expression, concentration, and liberation from constraints. There truly exists an inexhaustible range of sources at your disposal. When engaging in the process of modeling an individual, it is significantly more advantageous to utilize the presence of an actual person who can be observed in physical proximity. However, in this case, you are free to employ any exemplary figure as your guide, including but not limited to animated fictional characters. As an illustration, should you desire to cultivate a heightened level of sociability, you may opt for Bugs Bunny as a salient figure to emulate, as he may instill within you a sense of joviality.

First Step

Initially, select the comprehensive array of abilities you wish to cultivate. Alternatively, you may elucidate the circumstances in which you aspire to enhance your efficacy. This exercise embodies an experimental approach, encouraging you to engage in extensive iterations with a variety of characters, enabling you to discern the unique emotive responses they evoke. Subsequently, we will explore the process of identifying the four options that you wish to pursue and harnessing them for sustained educational development. Once you have determined the desired overarching characteristics (such as enhanced interpersonal abilities, improved academic techniques, enhanced imagination, etc.), proceed to select suitable exemplars.

Second Step

Exhibit the utmost level of creativity and unrestrained imaginative expression during this stage. Employ historical figures, characters from television or film, or animated characters. The sole stipulation is that they must manifest as a distinctly defined character, whether in the realm of reality or fiction. Having a greater understanding of them will prove advantageous. There should be an abundance of information readily accessible, which you can utilize to acquire knowledge about their subject. As an illustration, Genghis Khan could serve as a paradigm to emulate, irrespective of one's limited knowledge about him. Merely if you are inclined to engage in some research regarding his life and undertakings.

Third Step

Locate a suitable location in which you may enjoy uninhibited mobility. Choose a large room, or an open space where you can close your eyes and move around without worrying about calling attention to yourself. Establish a circular formation and dedicate sufficient time to removing any obstructions from the core of the circle. Utilize various breathing techniques, prayer methods, or visualization practices in order to imbue the circle with a sense of sacredness. Foster the notion that you occupy the core of this circle, wherein the space, time, and energy are infused with a profound state of latent power. It is imperative to envision this potential energy in a manner that resonates with utmost authenticity and plausibility. Conceive of the situation akin to the atmospheric prelude to a lightning discharge, or reminiscent of the electrically charged ambiance preceding the transient emergence of a time portal in the Terminator film franchise.

Fourth Step

Extend an invitation to the four entities residing beyond the confines of the present realm. Harness your profound reserves of vitality to summon them forth. Envision that each individual possesses a distinct sense of duty or calling to fulfill a greater purpose by venturing into your presence within this realm. Please envision this using any means at your disposal.

Fifth Step

Envision their arrival, individually taking their places within the circumference. Imagine they are first facing away from you, looking out across all time and space to further sanctify your holy circle and the exercise that is about to transpire. Please allow yourself ample time to envision each individual engaging in their personal meditation practice, diligently focusing on clearing their minds from any form of distraction.

Sixth Step

Once they have taken the necessary preparations, please grant them permission to turn and direct their attention towards you. Gradually rotate your body, directing your gaze towards each individual and maintaining eye contact with each one. Please close your eyes and envision the blending of their existence with your own. Envision absorbing the potent emotional impact that emanates from their actions, acquiring the corresponding attribute as a result. Devote ample time to each element, gradually rotating through the entire circumference.

Seventh Step

After incorporating all of these entities within yourself, proceed to engage in various breathing exercises, yoga techniques, or any other arcane disciplines that are familiar to you or that you are open to acquiring. The specific actions or methods employed are not of great significance; what truly matters is your selection and personalization of these techniques as an integral aspect of this undertaking.

How Long?

Upon establishing the relevant characters, allocate a minimum of ten minutes to complete the entire procedure. If feasible, endeavor to carry out this activity in an outdoor setting, endowed with natural ground such as grass or soil, as it will lend it a sense of authenticity and closeness to nature. In the event that the presence of an audience would hinder the proceedings, it is advisable to seek out a secluded space where your privacy can be ensured, thereby enabling you to freely manifest your thoughts and emotions.

Attempt with Alternative Individuals

Do not hesitate to experiment with various individuals to gauge your experience. Acknowledge that this is a form of illusion and by employing these metaphorical supporting characters, you are essentially compelling your mind to concentrate on four distinct emotional states consecutively. Certain combinations may not yield optimal results, whereas other combinations exhibit exceptional compatibility. Permit this to be a progressive undertaking, one that you can consider on a periodic basis.

Keep A Journal

Similar to other exercises of this nature, maintaining a journal documenting your experiences will prove to be highly beneficial. Allow yourself ample time to discover the optimal equilibrium of suitable individuals for the respective circumstances. Take your time with this task, for once you discover the appropriate arrangement of characters for various resources, you can consequently augment this further.

Reiterate using the most exceptional characters

Let us hypothesize that you have experimented with multiple permutations of character traits in order to enhance your social confidence. After achieving the appropriate blend, it is possible to engage in the same activity on a weekly basis using the identical set of four characters. There exist numerous possibilities for conceptualizing and executing it in diverse manners. On a weekly basis, it may be beneficial to experiment with incorporating various moments from their lives. Alternatively, with respect to an alternative specific objective.

Please ensure that you accompany them.

After acquiring familiarity with these identical characters, you will have the ability to carry them along with you. Consider the scenario where you are accompanied by these four fictional characters while attending social gatherings, such as club outings, with your companions. As you observe the gathered multitude, envisage every character proffering guidance to you. Alternatively, you have the option of permitting one or more of the characters to temporarily inhabit your being, providing you with a surge of self-assurance during times of necessity. One could envision the scenario where Don Draper, in a subdued manner, imparts guidance on the most effective approach to engage with a visually appealing woman situated at a distance within the vicinity.

Allow the Characters to Express Themselves through Your Journaling

This is an activity that can be experimented with while in a public setting. One can engage in the activity of sitting in a coffee shop and allowing each character to sequentially articulate their thoughts and sensations by means of journaling. Enabling or granting them the opportunity to write through you while you undergo the surrounding environment will afford you the ability to experiment with assorted mental states within familiar circumstances. For instance, when one finds themselves seated in a Starbucks establishment, amidst the presence of charming young women, while engaging in the act of journaling, adopting the persona of Genghis Khan, it is likely to provide an alternative and unique outlook. Abstain from engaging in any unlawful acts or participating in activities that may lead to subsequent remorse. When utilizing characters as aids for your educational enhancement, consider envisioning yourself studying alongside acclaimed intellectuals of history, perceiving their presence during the examination process. You are encouraged to exercise your creativity to the fullest extent with this task. There is no incorrect path or correct path; rather, there exists only what is effective and beneficial.

Natural Language Processing And The Management Of Weight Loss

However, it is important to note that NLP itself does not directly facilitate weight loss. Nonetheless, employing NLP techniques can prove beneficial in enhancing your dietary habits, ultimately aiding in the process of achieving weight loss in a more effortless manner. What would be the outcome if vegetables were to possess flavors reminiscent of confectioneries? What if the experience of engaging in physical exercise at the fitness center was significantly more enjoyable compared to remaining sedentary in bed throughout the day? Do you believe that weight reduction would continue to pose as an issue?

Losing weight cannot be achieved instantaneously. It is necessary to restrict energy usage to quantities lower than the amount being generated. The aforementioned concept can also be applied to NLP in regards to the management of weight loss. It is not feasible to assert that one will achieve weight loss through NLP and subsequently indulge in the consumption of a candy bar. However, it is possible to utilize NLP techniques to facilitate weight loss by altering the perception of a candy bar to make it less appealing.

Enhancing the Attractiveness of Nutritious Food through Natural Language Processing

The aforementioned principle can be extended to encompass all the nutritionally unfavorable food items that are not essential to consume, along with the foods that may lack personal appeal but are recognized as beneficial and should be incorporated into one's diet. Allow us to illustrate with broccoli as a case in point. Broccoli is an exceptionally nutritious food and highly encouraged for individuals aiming to lower their overall caloric consumption. Envision a scenario wherein each individual serving of fresh broccoli that you consume is assimilated by your body, thus contributing to a reduction in overall calorie intake.

Opting for a Visit to the Gym as Opposed to Remaining Sedentary on the Couch

The identical concept is applicable to this particular circumstance. In order to prioritize physical activity over a sedentary lifestyle, it is necessary to make subtle alterations to one's cognitive processes. Once again, it is entirely feasible and not particularly arduous if you apply focused mental effort.

When considering whether or not to engage in exercise, what is the initial thought that arises in your mind? Envision yourself engaging in the workout and contemplate the benefits you would derive from physical exertion. The response would likely entail "It would require a substantial amount of energy, effort, and a portion of my time." "It appears to require a significant amount of effort, which would result in considerable fatigue and bodily discomfort." Cease! Your thoughts are not being dictated by your brain! They are under your control.

When one admonishes oneself to engage in physical activity, an immediate mental image of successfully attaining a specific objective will be conjured. If you have yet to establish a goal, I recommend setting one promptly. Envision a scenario where you observe a visual representation of your future self, attaining the desired objective. How does it feel? Examine your visage more closely and take notice of your countenance. Gain a comprehensive understanding of the sensation of accomplishment through various outlooks. Consider the potential transformation that would occur in your life by implementing this change in a positive manner.

Utilizing Natural Language Processing (NLP) to Enhance the Enjoyment of Physical Activity

The utilization of visualization techniques proves highly efficacious in attaining one's objectives. It changes motivation. It proves to be efficacious during your exercise regimen as well.

What thoughts occupy your mind while engaging in activities such as running on a treadmill or lifting weights? You may be contemplating your disdain for the circumstances in which you find yourself. There is no justification for adopting such a thought process.

Rather, relish the sensation of the vitality coursing through your physical being. Take pleasure in the profound sense of life within you. Your body is operating on a significant magnitude. Experience the surge of hemoglobin coursing through your circulatory system, the intensified pulsations of your cardiac rhythm, and then celebrate in the euphoria. The momentary release of your body's inherent endorphins is rapidly increasing.

When engaging in physical activity, it is advisable to commence with modest objectives and gradually increase intensity in order to experience a sense of achievement. For instance, if you currently engage in physical activity for 10 minutes every two weeks, strive to increase your frequency to 10 minutes per week. Upon successful attainment, proceed to allocate 10 minutes for two sessions a week and subsequently escalate accordingly.

The Fundamental Assumptions Of Neuro Linguistic Programming

The 13 Golden Presuppositions serve as the fundamental tenets and philosophical foundations that underpin the field of Neuro Linguistic Programming. As such, these are the guiding principles and core ideas that must be understood, internalized and remembered by every practitioner of the discipline. As these ideas are commonly referred to as presuppositions, the most effective approach is to adopt the stance of assuming their truth and subsequently basing our actions on this assumption.

NLP Golden Presupposition # 1: Individuals React Based on Their Experiences

The initial foundational principle of Neuro-Linguistic Programming (NLP) posits that individuals may not invariably react to objective reality. On the contrary, individuals tend to be more receptive to their own personal encounters with objects, individuals, and circumstances.

The primary factor behind this phenomenon lies in the limited comprehension of individuals regarding the comprehensive scope of reality. Conversely, an individual can solely possess a conceptual representation of the world, influencing their conduct and attitudes based on their sensory perceptions, prior encounters, and cognitive frameworks. Due to the fact that individuals possess varying senses, past experiences, and belief systems, it is thereby rendered impossible for this map to ever achieve complete accuracy in representing the world.

The inherent connotation of this statement is that one lacks the ability to comprehend and familiarize oneself with the geographical region at hand. Therefore, it will be deemed that the depiction accurately represents the physical landscape. Given the diversity of individuals' backgrounds, it is evident that certain individuals possess more effective maps for attaining desired states or outcomes.

For the purpose of demonstrating, let us envision a scenario wherein existence is likened to safely maneuvering a vessel through treacherous waters in the Pacific Ocean. Although your personal map may not be entirely accurate, if it effectively identifies the most perilous locations (representing vices or activities that may lead to your downfall), you will navigate safely.

Nevertheless, if your personal map is severely flawed and rather than guiding you away from hazardous locations, it leads you directly towards them, then you are facing significant peril. The methodologies and tactics employed in the field of NLP are carefully tailored to facilitate the transformation of one's personal cognitive frameworks in a positive manner.

NLP Golden Presupposition #2: The Presence of Options

The second Golden Presupposition of NLP posits that the presence of options significantly surpasses the absence thereof. In accordance with the principles of Neuro-Linguistic Programming (NLP), it is advised to cultivate an individualized mental framework that facilitates a plethora of options. Hence, it is imperative that you consistently engage in behaviors that will result in an expansion of options within your personal sphere. Increased opportunities lead to greater personal liberation. Furthermore, as your level of freedom increases, so does your sphere of influence.

NLP Golden Presupposition #3: Individuals Exercise Optimal Decision-Making Capabilities

At a given juncture, individuals will invariably opt for the most optimal decision, thus constituting the third fundamental assumption of NLP. This implies that individuals consistently pursue their self-interest and opt for the most advantageous alternative or option regarding a particular matter or predicament. Nonetheless, it must be acknowledged that their decision may not necessarily be deemed as accurate;

their viewpoint regarding their optimal choices remains constrained by their flawed and restricted personal perspectives. Hence, it would be advisable to furnish them with an improved individualized roadmap.

NLP Golden Presupposition # 4: Individuals function flawlessly.

The fourth fundamental assumption in the field of Neuro-Linguistic Programming (NLP) postulates that every individual strives for excellence in their actions. Consequently, each individual effectively implements their methodologies, blueprints, and tactics flawlessly. The issue stems from the deficiency and undesirability inherent in their technique, plan, and strategy. Consequently, this is the underlying cause for why their endeavors may fail to yield a successful outcome (desired outcome).

NLP Golden Presupposition # 5: Actions Driven by Intention

The fifth fundamental assumption of NLP posits that there exists a underlying purpose driving every action undertaken or carried out by every individual. This implies that actions are not executed or performed haphazardly. Alternatively, actions are imbued with intent, motivations, and purpose, whether they are executed knowingly or unknowingly. This objective perpetually consists of endeavors that hold intrinsic worth or yield advantages to the individual in question.

The sixth presupposition of NLP states that every behavior is driven by a positive intention.

The sixth principle of NLP, known as the Golden Presupposition, denotes that every behavior is driven by an underlying positive intention. This implies that individuals, in any set of available options, will consistently select and dedicate themselves to pursuing the course of action that effectively fulfills their underlying favorable objective.

NLP Golden Presupposition #7: The unconscious mind strives to maintain equilibrium between the conscious and unconscious realms.

The seventh Golden Presupposition of NLP posits that the human mind possesses all the requisite abilities and assets necessary to accomplish the envisioned state or objective. The employed mind possesses all the available assets in current time, whereas the subconscious mind harbors all the elements not currently within the former domain.

The significance of response in effective communication, as per NLP Golden Presupposition # 8, cannot be overlooked.

The eighth fundamental principle in the field of NLP dictates that the primary objective of engaging in interpersonal communication with individuals is to elicit a corresponding reaction or feedback. Indeed, it is accurate to state that the reaction received from the individual in question may not align with one's preferred response. However, it is imperative to acknowledge that within the realm of Neuro Linguistic

Programming, the concept of communication failure does not exist. On the contrary, feedback or response would only yield unsuccessful outcomes. Put simply, should the response you receive not align with your desired outcome, it becomes necessary to alter and refine the manner in which you communicate with the individual in question.

Ninth Presupposition of NLP: The necessary resources are easily accessible.

The ninth principle of NLP, known as the Golden Presupposition, posits that each individual possesses all the requisite resources necessary to navigate through life effectively. This implies that individuals who appear to have limited resources are potentially hindered by their insufficient ability to effectively harness and exploit available resources due to a lack of creativity.

NLP Golden Presupposition #10: The mind and body manifest as distinct aspects of an individual.

The notion held in the tenth Golden Presupposition of NLP is that the human mind and body exist as distinct manifestations of an individual. Through reciprocal interaction and mutual influence, the intellect and the physique establish a cohesive and integrated entity. Due to the inseparable connection between the mind and the body, any alteration to one invariably leads to corresponding modifications in the other.

In actuality, altering one's cognitive perspective regarding an issue or problem leads to corresponding physiological transformations within the body, thereby eliciting dissimilar sensations and emotions. On the contrary, when one behaves in a distinct manner (pertaining to bodily functions) towards an individual, collective, setting, or circumstance, there is a subtle transformation of one's thoughts and emotions (pertaining to mental processes).

NLP Golden Presupposition # 11: The processing of information occurs through the sensory faculties.

The eleventh Golden Presupposition of NLP posits that each individual perceives and interprets all information through their sensory faculties. Hence, in order to obtain enhanced and more pragmatic knowledge, enhance cognitive clarity, and acquire a more refined internal perception, it is imperative to consistently nurture your senses, rendering them more receptive and perceptive to the external realm.

NLP Golden Presupposition #12: Engaging in the Study and Replication of Effective Performance

The twelfth Golden Presupposition of NLP posits that in order to attain excellence, one must emulate the actions, attitudes, and behaviors of individuals who have achieved success. The underlying principle of this presupposition suggests that if a person has accomplished something, it is equally feasible for others to achieve the same outcome by cultivating a mindset grounded in self-belief. Put differently, it is imperative that you draw lessons from the experiences of those who have preceded you.

NLP Presumption of Significance 13: Engage in Action for the Purpose of Comprehension

The thirteenth Golden Presupposition of NLP states that in order to gain comprehension of something, it is imperative to engage in an action that facilitates understanding. The underlying rationale for this assumption rests on the notion that one cannot acquire knowledge or skills through inactivity. Therefore, it is imperative to consistently conduct oneself and acquire practical knowledge in order to acquire comprehension and insight. As commonly expressed, experience serves as the paramount educator.

Official Neuro-Linguistic Guide

After perusing the "official neurolinguistic guide" provided by the DVNLP, one may ascertain that NLP is founded upon the discoveries of contemporary linguistics, systems theory, psychology, and neurophysiology. Natural Language Processing (NLP) thus encompasses fundamental procedures. These include:

- The manner in which a man views himself,

- Independently handles the analysis of these findings.

- Executes actions based on this premise,

- Engages in effective communication with peers,

- Acquires knowledge and undergoes transformation.

Every individual possesses a distinctive method of addressing their personal matters and specific circumstances. This encompasses interpersonal interactions, professional pursuits, interpersonal bonds, and all the phenomena typically encountered throughout one's personal journey. The way you perceive yourself and your surroundings at a specific moment can shape your emotions and the evaluation of the circumstances. Consequently, you might perceive the identical circumstance as enjoyable and gratifying, or alternatively, as demanding and arduous.

In the field of Natural Language Processing (NLP), researchers employ studies and frameworks pertaining to the perception and processing of information. These endeavors aim to discern the determining factors, influences, and contextual factors that govern an individual's personal encounters while also elucidating the mechanisms underlying the generation of these experiences. Based on this underlying premise, a plethora of action methods have been formulated over the course of the previous decades.

The NLP techniques possess a practical focus and are advantageous for personal growth and enhancing interpersonal communication. Within the realm of behavioral and cognitive science, the discipline of NLP assumes the role of exploring the subjective aspects of human experience and leveraging these insights to present individuals, groups, or organizations with an array of adaptable prospects for effecting purposeful transformations and resolutions. In line with the broader scientific realm, research findings contribute to ongoing advancements.

Neuro-linguistic programming serves to elevate one's understanding of the diverse processes that impact their personal encounters. As a consequence, this leads to a heightened utilization of the five senses and an individual's innate capabilities. This enables the formulation of more precise goals by considering one's influencing factors during the realization process. Because of the continuous growth of information in recent years, individuals engaging in professional discourse have the privilege to...

In order to enhance their comprehension of interpersonal communication processes,

To accommodate the interlocutor's perspective while disregarding the reliance on one's own content and methodological orientation.

To significantly enhance your engagement with individuals"

• To approach the challenges and daily fluctuations with great adaptability.

Diverse viewpoints when contemplating Natural Language Processing (NLP) "Diverse standpoints in relation to NLP analysis "Varied outlooks when examining the field of NLP "Alternative angles to consider within the realm of NLP"

Individuals who possess an inclination towards neuro-linguistic programming, engage in conversations with experts and delve into pertinent scholarly resources, will promptly discern the intricately varying and diverse nature of the descriptions. The various delineations are derived from a comprehensive methodology encompassing a broad spectrum. The subsequent viewpoints are thus taken into account in the context of Natural Language Processing (NLP).

Neuro-linguistic programming encompasses the processes of comprehending, articulating, and engaging in effective dialogue.

The notion that individuals consistently engage in communication is a fundamental tenet of NLP. This not only encompasses verbal communication. Furthermore, it encompasses nonverbal cues such as the countenance, movements, vocal inflection, body positioning, and myriad additional elements." Hence, the inquiry arises regarding the manner in which individuals communicate and its modalities. Can you effectively articulate your thoughts in a manner that ensures comprehension by the individual with whom you are conversing? Is there any evidence to suggest that the individual with whom you are engaged in conversation has comprehended the information conveyed to them?

In what manner can these clues be utilized? If one has achieved proficiency in neuro-linguistic programming, one can leverage a diverse array of techniques to facilitate effective communication.

Neuro-linguistic programming pertains to the study and utilization of language.

The manner in which individuals communicate has a substantial impact on their cognition and response patterns. The ability to compress and represent experiences is necessary in order to convey the knowledge and wisdom that you transmit through language. It is imperative that you articulate your perception of the surroundings through verbal means, consequently leading to the distortion of the image. Consequently, crucial information remains uncommunicated to the interlocutor.

Neuro-linguistic programming equips individuals with beneficial frameworks and probing methodologies to mold dialogues and introspective interactions in alignment with their desires. You will acquire a comprehensive comprehension of how the utilization of language exerts influence over one's cognition and behavior. Language possesses a profound capacity to subtly shape one's premonitions, akin to treacherous traps that lie in wait, amplifying the significance of our choice in words. It would be beneficial if you could refrain from doing so. If instructed to abstain from contemplating delectable, savory cuisine, it is likely that your cognitions will solely fixate upon the repast. The careful selection of language yielded precisely the opposite outcome! When engaging in communication, it is imperative to be mindful of the implicit assumptions conveyed by our choice of words, particularly the impact of employing the term 'but'. A minor illustration: "I have an appreciation for the dish you prepared, however..."

The conversational participant frequently overlooks the initial clause due to an anticipatory inclination towards subsequent expressions conveying negation. Examine the advertisement practices in media outlets and analyze the oratory skills utilized by politicians. They employ a distinct linguistic code through which messages are conveyed and firmly established in the minds of the recipients. The stimuli that enter into consciousness can be identified using NLP. This outcome leads to a form of safeguarding for their mental faculties.

6. Picture Frame Technique

The 'Picture Frame' methodology provides a successful means of relinquishing negative memories and experiences that diminish your self-worth and engender feelings of discontent. By utilizing this methodology, you have the ability to dispel any unfavorable emotions associated with undesirable circumstances, such as the termination of a romantic relationship, unemployment, or any other comparable situations that elicit sorrow and distress.

Mastering the Art of Utilizing the Picture Frame Technique

"Allow me to elucidate the procedural intricacies of implementing this technique:

1. Consider any unfavorable encounter in which you wish to alter your perspective or one that fills you with a sense of self-doubt, and mentally capture its essence. For example, if you still find yourself feeling distressed over the end of your relationship, and the memory of that experience continues to weigh on you, hold on to that recollection and capture it in a visual representation. Ensure that you are included in that captured image.

2. Envision beholding that photograph from a detached, observer's standpoint.

3. Examine your emotional response to the image. Does gazing upon it elicit unpleasant recollections of that event?

4. If you answer affirmatively, kindly convert the aforementioned snapshot into a monochrome image, intentionally

reducing the picture's clarity slightly, and applying any desired filters such as sepia tone. Does the image still evoke unpleasant emotions within you? It is probable that by this point in time, the negative sentiment should have diminished.

5. If the image continues to cause distress, envision augmenting it with a Snapchat filter. If one is actively engaged in social media, they would likely be familiar with the significance of this. Apply any humorous filter to the image, such as altering the nasal dimensions, incorporating a mustache, or transforming into a deer. By engaging in this activity, you will begin to experience a sense of emotional well-being when gazing upon the image.

6. Feel free to incorporate an elegant or vintage frame into the design. Envision this artwork displayed within the confines of an art gallery. Consider the scenario of numerous individuals strolling by and appreciating this exquisite mural.

7. What are your current sentiments regarding the aforementioned picture and the linked occasion? It is probable that the negative sentiment would have subsided at this point.

The picture frame technique aids in reframing an adverse event ingrained in the subconscious mind, allowing it to be regarded purely as a static image. By perceiving a negative memory as a thing of the past and a vivid image in your mind, that memory ceases to cause you distress. Experiment with this approach on various other distressing memories that you wish to attain emotional relief from, and observe the expeditious evaporation of your suffering.

NLP possesses the capacity to not solely facilitate a shift in your emotional perception of distressing experiences, but additionally foster heightened engagement in your professional endeavors, through the synthesis of disparate emotional states. The technique of "Visual Squash" is an ideal method to accomplish this objective.

Allow us to acquire knowledge regarding its nature and implications in the subsequent section.

7. Visual Squash Technique

The 'Visual Squash' is a remarkable NLP technique that facilitates cognitive reframing to encourage a shift in one's patterns of thinking. Frequently, we encounter circumstances that evoke a sense of perplexity in regards to our course of action and the methodology to be employed.

Maybe you had intended to prioritize an important task, yet an alternate inclination compelled you to indulge in sleep or engage in a more captivating activity. In such circumstances, we frequently give consideration to the aspect that offers a more captivating or calming alternative. This, nevertheless, has an impact on our efficiency.

If you do not want to give in to temptations, want to be more focused and alert, and always want to make your mind work the way you want it to, the visual squash technique is perfect for you.

The application of the visual squash technique in natural language processing enables the synthesis of disparate concepts, emotional states, or recommendations to yield an enhanced and expanded outcome. For example, should you desire to derive satisfaction from accomplishing a time-critical task, the implementation of the visual squash technique can assist you in discovering a more pleasurable approach to task completion, thereby enhancing your propensity to engage in the work willingly and effortlessly. Allow us to ascertain the methods by which you may engage in its practice.

Mastering the Visual Squash Technique: A Guide to Effective Practice

Here is a step-by-step guide on how to effectively engage in practicing this NLP technique:

1. Please consider the issue upon which you wish to focus your efforts. If one frequently engages in procrastination and desires to overcome it, one may employ the technique of visualizing oneself deferring completion of a significant task.

2. Extend either your left or right hand before you, and visualize grasping that problematic state within your hand.

3. Generate a graphical depiction of the aforementioned state of the problem. In light of this, it is imperative that you perceive, detect, discern, experience, and observe the current state of the problem. Pursuing with the preceding illustration, should you be deferring a crucial undertaking, you might experience a sense of heaviness associated with it. Envision procrastination as a vast abyss into which you descend, exuding an alarming cacophony, exerting a weighty burden, emitting an unpleasant odor,

and leaving an unfavorable taste akin to mud or repugnant substances.

4. Consider any emotion you desire to experience in its place. If you aspire to cultivate a heightened sense of enthusiasm towards your work, thereby enabling you to channel your concentration, consider contemplating this aspiration.

5. Please proceed to extend your alternate hand outwards, envisioning the esteemed condition being cradled within its grasp. Additionally, generate a graphical depiction of it. For example, it may resemble an exquisite container replete with extraordinary contents, providing a delightful tactile experience, emitting a pleasing auditory sensation, exhibiting a jelly-like flavor when tasted, and emanating a fragrance reminiscent of roses.

6. Once you have effectively and meticulously envisaged the specific state you desire, proceed to alternately oscillate between your hands. Continuously direct your attention

towards your issue and subsequently towards the intended goal. Please perform the task between 5 and 10 repetitions.

7. Very slowly bring both your hands closer together and hold them. This effectively consolidates and unifies the two states. Now contemplate your sentiments regarding the assignment you were procrastinating on earlier. It is probable that you will experience a distinct sense of excitement and may have even stumbled upon an intriguing approach to accomplish the task as well.

8. Place your hands upon any region of your body, such as your chest, and proceed to gently massage the area. You have firmly secured that state within the confines of your heart. Now, when the inclination toward procrastination arises, clasping your hands against your chest will foster a heightened sense of enthusiasm toward engaging in the task at hand.

Consistently engage in the practice of this technique until you achieve mastery.

Additionally, it can be utilized to transform one's diminished self-confidence into a robust sense of self-worth, to convert feelings of unhappiness or dissatisfaction into contentment, and to employ dual proficiency in acquiring novel knowledge.

As an example, one might consider blending their aptitude for creativity with the desire to apply their imaginative capabilities towards the accomplishment of monotonous duties. By amalgamating these two facets, one could potentially devise a novel means of executing mundane tasks.

This method facilitates the alteration of one's perception towards mundane experiences or the amalgamation of disparate entities to generate a more entertaining outcome. An alternative methodology known as the "grid" technique can assist individuals in overcoming their phobias, temptations, and resistances. The subsequent section proceeds to explicate that technique extensively.

Adopting a Practice of Mindful Eating:

Effecting a change in a deeply entrenched habit requires conscious effort and cannot be accomplished spontaneously. The automatic behavioral patterns and actions we engage in occur within the regions of our brains that operate independently of conscious thought. To effectuate the reprogramming of these entrenched cognitive patterns, it is imperative to be consistently reinforced. This is the sole means by which you shall relinquish your former patterns of behavior. "Presented herein are a set of initial approaches to accomplish the aforementioned objective:

- Employing Repetition for Transformation: In order to establish a new, improved pattern, it is imperative to consistently practice the desired behavior. Despite the availability of numerous techniques and methods to aid in this matter, the degree to which you can diligently adhere to them for a minimum duration of one month will greatly influence the outcome of your endeavors.

• Place Emphasis on a Limited Number of Habits: The primary principle here is to direct your attention towards no more than two new habits (or fewer) simultaneously. For instance, it is possible to observe one's appetite prior to eating and make a conscious decision to engage in more meticulous chewing. Rather than becoming overwhelmed by a completely different perspective on food, this approach facilitates improved concentration and focus.

• Memo: Commence by strategically placing reminders in highly visible locations that you are likely to encounter at regular intervals during the course of your day. This can be positioned either on your office desk, your refrigerator, or your vehicle's steering wheel. Please ensure that you express these affirmative statements in the present tense, for example, "I consistently engage in the thorough chewing of my mouthfuls of food." On each occasion that you come across one of these notes, pause your current activities and give it thoughtful consideration.

- Seek a Collaborator: The synergistic effect of having a fellow participant to hold you accountable can serve as a valuable asset in your pursuit of weight loss. By engaging in a dialogue regarding your intentions with a companion, you are fortifying your determination, fostering mutual encouragement, and mutually upholding the commitment to the altered behavioral patterns.

- Pardon Errors: It is often effortless to chastise oneself upon falling short of adhering to one's personal commitments regarding healthier decision-making. Please bear in mind that this approach is regrettably unproductive and will ultimately hinder your progress further. To maintain perseverance, it is advisable to exude self-kindness during moments of failure, while keeping in mind that one's efforts are directed towards personal improvement, which is indeed commendable.

NLP Strategies for Establishing a Mindful Approach to Eating Habits:

Fortunately, systematic procedures exist for addressing unconscious eating habits. In the following section, we will be discussing three NLP exercises that you can commence implementing at present.

Method 1: Establishing Communication with the Neural Signals Emitted by Your Brain

It is quite effortless to consume an excessive amount, particularly when indulging in a delectable feast. However, this inevitably gives rise to feelings of discomfort, a sense of bloating, and ultimately, an increase in body weight. Acquiring knowledge about the various signals that your brain transmits during meals, along with acquiring the ability to consciously recognize and interpret them, is imperative for the purpose of weight reduction. How can one determine the point at which satiety is reached and it is appropriate to discontinue consumption?

Developing Effective Listening Skills: For certain individuals, calorie monitoring may appear to be the foremost pivotal measure towards weight loss and attaining mastery over one's eating patterns. However, our physiological systems are inherently designed to accurately regulate our satiety signals. To alter your approach to food, it is imperative to start attentively heeding the signals from your body indicating satiety. There is no longer a necessity for the excessive and psychologically draining activity of counting calories.

● Comprehending Satiety: The capacity of our stomachs is approximately 17 cups of food. Notwithstanding, sensations of satiety do not arise from the stomach achieving fullness. Instead, our sensation of fullness emerges as a result of our brains reacting to the chemical composition of the substances we ingest. The cognitive process of the brain necessitates approximately 20 minutes to align with and respond to this stimulus. After concluding your meal, this sensation intensifies for a duration of approximately thirty minutes. Subsequently, they will maintain an elevated level for a duration of up to five hours, with the aim of ensuring satiety. Once these levels decrease, the sensation of hunger emerges.

It is important to exercise patience and refrain from making conclusions about satiety until the consumption of the entire meal has concluded. In many instances, it is a common occurrence for your appetite to diminish after approximately 20 minutes, once your cognitive faculties have fully processed the sensation. Consequently, there may be no necessity to consume further sustenance, even if your initial inclination suggested otherwise.

• Observe Your Stomach Sensations: Begin to monitor the sensations you experience when you feel hungry, as well as the sensations following water consumption. One shall observe that the sensation of void within the abdominal region diminishes subsequent to the consumption of a glass of water. When you partake in a meal in the future, contemplate the sensations experienced by your digestive system during the act of ingesting. Upon reaching a state of satiety, one will become aware of a subtle pressure that supplants the previous feelings of emptiness and hunger. Upon observation of this, discontinue consumption promptly. This will enable you to maintain a sense of vitality and a feeling of lightness subsequent to consuming your meal. If, at any given moment, you find yourself experiencing discomfort as a result of excessive pressure, it indicates that you have consumed an excessive amount.

"Additional Resources for Incorporating Mindful Eating Practices:

- Water Intake: It is recommended to consume a full glass of water 15 minutes prior to each meal. As a consequence, your brain will perceive satiety within a mere 10 minutes as opposed to the previous duration of 20 minutes. Please replenish your glass and consume an additional complete glass of beverage while partaking in your meal, ensuring to intermittently pause and sip. This will impede your progress.

- Mastication: The majority of individuals do not engage in adequate mastication of their food, resulting in stomach discomfort, digestive disturbances, and, inevitably, an increase in body weight. This notion prompts us to consider that we ought to consume an amount greater than what is truly necessary. In order to effectively address this unfavorable behavior, it is imperative to consciously chew each morsel of food no less than 15 times. Once you have achieved a state of satiety, promptly store the remaining portion of nourishment and engage in alternative activities like pursuing a hobby, embarking on a walk, or engaging in conversation with your spouse.

- Coffee or Tea: If you find it challenging to resist the urge to continue eating, prepare some coffee or unsweetened tea as an interim solution. Refrain from consuming additional food unless your appetite resurfaces. The sensations experienced prior to your body's actual need for nourishment are a product of cognitive rather than physiological processes.

- During meal times, focus solely on eating: Establish a personal guideline in which you dedicate your full concentration to the act of eating, rather than diverting attention towards television or work-related correspondence. Furthermore, it is advisable to cultivate an air of formality when it comes to partaking in meals, by choosing to sit at a dining table rather than reclining on a couch or consuming food within a vehicle.

- Foster an Appreciation for Flavors: Dedicate a portion of your time to actively savoring and discerning the various subtleties in the food you consume, while contemplating the nutritional benefits it provides. Adopt a mindset characterized by gratitude and appreciation towards this activity, refraining from perceiving eating merely as a basic necessity or source of pleasure. This intervention has the potential to significantly alter and improve your relationship with sustenance. Eventually, you will become less likely to indulge yourself too often and start viewing food as nourishment, not entertainment.

Adhering to all of the aforementioned recommendations will enable your body to attain its inherent, optimal weight. Furthermore, our bodily mechanisms inherently possess the ability to discern our hunger cues, satiety levels, and the dispensability of a second serving. The crucial aspect lies in attuning oneself to the inherent wisdom that already resides within.

Enhancing Vocal And Physical Confidence: A Comprehensive Guide

In the forthcoming exercise, we shall be implementing a novel approach, a fresh methodology aimed at fostering a profound sense of self-assurance within you.

In this particular exercise, we will be employing the utilization of your vocal faculties to modify your voice into one that exudes self-assurance, simultaneously bolstering your physical demeanor to a state of confidence. Now, kindly accompany me as I provide guidance for this exercise. Please be advised that you may choose to undertake this exercise either with your eyes closed or open, while ensuring that no interruptions will occur for the duration of the following 15 minutes.

So get ready now. Now, I ask you to contemplate an individual whose vocal presence you find appealing and hold in high esteem. Think about someone. He has the potential to serve as your acquaintance, your professional associate, or an entertainer in the film industry or a sports professional. It can be anybody. And observe their vocal quality, what aspects of their voice do you particularly appreciate? What aspects about their voice do you find admirable? Observe the demeanor, the pace of their speech, and their conduct. Just notice. One can envision them as if they are being heard in the present moment. Now, I urge you to mentally assimilate their spoken words. Recalling the most recent occasion on which you encountered that information, it could be through a conversation, radio, or television. Continue to listen attentively, repeatedly examining their voice until you have acquired a comprehensive understanding of its distinct attributes. Be aware of it. Notice it. And now, get a newspaper or magazine and start reading an article in your mind. Please be reminded to internally read the text, refraining from vocalizing it. Employing the gentle, mellifluous tones reminiscent of an individual held in high regard. Envision the sound resonating within your thoughts while observing the words upon the page with your eyes. Do it now. One may commence by constructing a few sentences and subsequently reiterating them until a sense of mastery is achieved. The auditory perception is originating from within your cranial cavity. Upon perusing those written expressions, one cannot help but evoke the individual whom you had envisioned, the very one towards whom you are emulating yourself. Please feel free to take all the time you need. You are welcome to pause your progress in this course and engage in the exercise at hand. Resume when you feel prepared to continue.

Commence the task of audibly reciting those identical sentences once more. Aligning your vocal qualities with those of the other person. Continuously reflect on that internal dialogue while articulating your thoughts aloud. Repeat this several times. Practice repeatedly until you achieve mastery.

Take note of how your own voice gradually aligns itself with the internal voice. What did you change? What mix it better? What works? What does not work? Tick the lessons. It is advisable to practice this exercise repeatedly, as it will facilitate your understanding of the necessary steps one must take to enhance the confidence and appeal of your voice, resulting in a potential improvement that may surpass previous achievements. Engage in additional repetitions of the exercise before progressing forward.

Now you are employing your cognitive faculties to enhance your physical assurance. We have all encountered individuals whose confidence is evident upon first glance. Their assuredness is conveyed through their gait, body language, hand movements, posture, the graceful motions of their hair, and the twinkle in their eyes. What qualities do they possess that give you the impression of confidence? What sets them apart from their peers. Just notice that.

Now contemplate an individual who exerts such an influence upon you. I kindly request that you consider an individual whom you perceive as possessing a notable level of self-assurance. Observe their gait, physical demeanor, and manual expressions. An individual who exudes an air of self-assurance upon a mere glance. It may consist of individuals with whom you have a personal acquaintance, coworkers, acquaintances, or individuals who may have been encountered through televised or cinematic mediums. Now, I kindly request that you rise from your seat and envision the presence of that individual directly before you. Very close to you. Please carefully observe them. Observe the manner in which they exhibit movement, their nonverbal cues, and their bodily postures. Visualize this image before you, enhancing its vibrancy, intensity, and intricacy. Take meticulous note of every minute detail that characterizes the individual.

Now, I would like to propose an intriguing idea: I encourage you to envision yourself inhabiting the physical form of that individual. How might one have experienced such a situation if they were in your position? Observe their thoughts, emotions, and actions, as well as your own body language and posture while inhabiting their perspective. Acquire knowledge about their bodily movements, discern their internal thoughts, and assume their perspective by physically advancing, exploring the surroundings, and discerning the level of confidence experienced through such movements. Now, proceed to derive knowledge from that particular situation and observe the methods in which they utilize their movements.

What measures do they take to bolster their self-assurance? Take note of the aspects that necessitate alterations in your nonverbal communication. Utilize the knowledge acquired during that process, and once you experience that remarkable sensation within your body, the sensation of confidence, proceed to recreate the same anchoring technique performed in the previous exercise. Place your thumb and middle finger on the hand you predominantly use, apply pressure, and silently affirm in your thoughts, "I am confident." I possess a profound sense of assurance, which, in turn, serves to activate the anchor within your physical being. In the event that you require this self-assured sensation at any point in the forthcoming days, simply apply pressure to your thumb and middle finger on your dominant hand while silently affirming the phrase 'I am confident' within your thoughts. Immediately, an overwhelming sense of confidence will permeate your entire being, fostering an extraordinary level of self-assurance. Employ this methodology, in order to elicit a state of assurance in any desired location, at any given time, according to your discretion. Simply contemplate this trigger, create this trigger, and attempt it by applying pressure to the thumb and middle finger of your dominant hand while mentally uttering the word, "I am assured." Immediately, a sense of assertiveness envelops both your physical and mental state.

Ladies and gentlemen, throughout this course, you have acquired knowledge pertaining to the functioning of the human mind, the utilization of cognitive faculties, the nuances of both positive and negative memory, and their impact on your individual experiences. You have acquired the ability to articulate three positive occurrences experienced within a day and have successfully established a catalyst for boosting self-assurance. In the preceding exercise, you acquired the knowledge of utilizing vocal techniques to enhance self-assurance, adeptly modulate your voice, and exhibit poised body language. Therefore, I strongly encourage you to revisit this course and engage in the exercises several more times, in order to solidify the concepts and knowledge you have acquired. Furthermore, as you continue to engage in the exercise, your confidence will progressively grow. Your cognitive state will attain an exceptional level of confidence, prompting you to embody a compelling persona characterized by unwavering self-assurance. So, my companions, I extend my heartfelt wishes for your utmost prosperity and triumph. I anticipate the opportunity to meet you in the near future. Do the exercises.

Conduct Calibration Solely Based On Behavior

This presupposition varies from the second one, which states that individuals should not be defined solely by their actions.

As sentient individuals, we possess the ability to ascertain a person's character through their behavior, thereby allowing us to gain insight into their experiences or difficulties.

On certain occasions, individuals may make promises, yet fail to demonstrate commitment in their actions. Therefore, it is your conviction that one's actions speak louder than their words.

The course of action that you should undertake:

One should refrain from solely relying on verbal communication to comprehend an individual's nature; instead, it is imperative to observe and analyze their actions in order to truly grasp their character. However, it is advised to refrain from making judgments solely based on his actions, but rather endeavor to assess him by examining his conduct.

This should not imply that one should pass judgement on individuals based solely on their behavior, as articulated in presupposition 2, wherein it is acknowledged that a person's behavior does not define their entire persona.

If you are a coach or a mentor, or hold a position of providing guidance instead of inquiring about one's struggles or negative emotions, kindly inquire about their actions and habits.

"The advantages that you will receive:

You possess a natural aptitude for comprehending individuals, rather than passing judgment upon them.

You shall not be inclined to naivety, as you will refrain from assessing individuals based on their words or outward appearances.

Engaging in these activities will cultivate a formidable and resolute character, as well as impart sagacity, as you develop the discernment and insight to accurately assess and comprehend individuals.

You will be a valuable asset as you possess insights into the voids in individuals' lives, recognizing the limitation of self-disclosure in one's self-representation.

Presumption 8: Individuals are not flawed or damaged:

The meaning:

It is important to emphasize that you are not broken. I reiterate this point: you are not broken. It is understandable that you may hold a different perspective at present, and it is worth acknowledging that this belief contradicts various principles in psychology and philosophy. However, it is important to note that individuals may present varying opinions in response to your declaration that you are not broken. And there is a significant number of highly qualified mental health professionals including therapists, psychologists, psychiatrists, and counselors who may employ the strategy of fostering the notion of personal inadequacy to encourage repeated attendance in sessions, thereby maximizing their financial gains.

To be candid, my purpose here is not to persuade you, as the initial presupposition establishes that the map does not represent the territory accurately, implying that my beliefs do not necessarily align with yours. I kindly request that you direct your attention to the ensuing sentences and contemplate whether this presupposition is beneficial to you. If that is not the case, you retain the freedom to hold your own beliefs, and naturally, this principle applies to all presuppositions of NLP.

Therefore, it can be inferred that you are indeed not fractured, rather what is being conveyed is that a substantial portion of the suffering you experience stems from psychological constructions within your consciousness. In reality, over 90% of the pain you experience is solely fabricated. Upon observing your external circumstances, it becomes evident that you lead a prosperous existence, surpassing the standards of many individuals in your immediate vicinity. Simply observe those individuals who lack adequate housing and those who are unable to access sufficient nourishment.

Your persistent issue lies in your tendency to constantly perceive those who possess more than you. Consequently, you engage in comparisons between yourself and these individuals, which subsequently leads your mind to adopt the belief that you are deficient due to lacking what they possess. Interestingly enough, it is noteworthy that individuals who do not possess the same resources as yourself tend to experience a sense of inadequacy due to their lack thereof.

When an individual believes they are broken, they are merely holding onto a false perception of their own identity, as they are in fact whole. This detrimental belief can be characterized as limiting and harmful.

The recommended course of action:

It is advisable that you refrain from adopting a victim's mindset. It would be advisable to cease incessantly expressing discontent towards matters that do not warrant complaint, as they solely exist within the realm of your imagination. And conjecture not, for it is an unfortunate circumstance that the individuals to whom you lament are themselves beset with afflictions, rendering them unable to render assistance in the majority of instances. It is not suggested that one should refrain from expressing their emotions and distress to others. However, it is advisable to refrain from voicing grievances about nonexistent circumstances or issues solely perceived within one's own thoughts.

Occasionally, engaging in complaints and adopting a victim mindset can exacerbate one's circumstances as it perpetuates the notion of personal inadequacy, thereby impeding progress in life.

Furthermore, it is imperative to refrain from fixating on the possessions and accomplishments of others, and subsequently comparing one's own blessings to those who have been bestowed with greater blessings. As a result of this situation, your sense of contentment will be completely extinguished, perpetuating a constant state of dependence and leading to relentless bouts of sorrow throughout both day and night due to the absence of this particular object. Alternatively, express appreciation for what you possess, irrespective of its magnitude. Express gratitude for all that you possess, including the wisdom gained from life's trials and tribulations...

Are you aware that your ego can be antagonistic to your progress? Due to the presence of your ego, you maintain a belief that you are afflicted and in greater need of assistance than any individual on this planet. Moreover, your inflated self-importance leads you to harbor the belief that you are entitled to greater possessions and a superior lifestyle compared to your friends or acquaintances. Consequently, when you are unable to attain these aspirations, you experience a sense of emotional distress and despondency. You must refrain from displaying excessive egotism and bear in mind that having an inflated ego will not benefit you in any way.

On certain occasions, rather than expressing dissatisfaction over lacking something, endeavor to attain that which you desire and establish it as an objective to pursue. Remember that your actions will ultimately dictate your destination and the possessions you will acquire. However, it is important to bear in mind that your aspirations should not originate from a place of self-centredness, where your sole objective is to attain achievements for the purpose of grandstanding. Additionally, it is essential that your ambitions reflect your own desires rather than being influenced by your parents or societal expectations. It is crucial to refrain from pursuing a profession, such as being a doctor, solely based on parental coercion. Instead, strive to accomplish objectives that resonate with your personal fulfillment and cultivate genuine happiness within you.

On occasion, individuals may encounter significant mental health concerns that necessitate assistance; consequently, seeking aid from a qualified professional becomes imperative. However, it is essential to understand that you have the capacity to overcome this situation, to achieve wellness. It is crucial to recognize that you are not inherently flawed or damaged by external circumstances; rather, you simply require assistance to make progress and navigate through life successfully.

Dissociation: Detach Yourself From Adverse Encounters

Allow us to familiarize ourselves with an additional potent technique that enables the alleviation of the intensity of previous adverse encounters, altering their framework, and consequently liberating oneself from the confines of a restricted, diminished perception of reality, thus infusing it with fresh hues and prospects. This method is commonly referred to as dissociation.

Envisage a delightful scenario from your personal experiences. Please keep in mind the visual, auditory, and kinesthetic cues. Please answer the following inquiry: At what location do you find yourself envisioning this particular situation? Are you immersed within it, or do you observe it from a peripheral vantage point, akin to a viewer in a theater or cinema, or as if you are scrutinizing a photograph?

If one perceives the visual representation of the occurrence from an internal perspective, as though one were situated within the very circumstances, assuming an active role in the event, and experiencing renewed concern or anxiety as though it is presently unfolding - an associative image is formed.

Association - a mental state characterized by utmost engagement in an event (or its recollection), whereby one experiences it from within and vividly re-experiences all the attendant emotions.

By adopting an observer perspective and mentally detaching oneself from a particular situation, one can effectively create a dissociated image. Dissociation is an altered state wherein one appears to disengage from a given circumstance, perceiving it (or the recollection thereof) from an external perspective, akin to that of a passive observer, effectively segregating the situational context from the accompanying emotional experiences.

Please be advised that when analyzing the situation from an external perspective, one effectively distances oneself from it. You are hereby excluded from participation. You have transitioned into the role of a mere external observer. Although you may have previously been actively involved in events, in the present moment, you have the ability to distance yourself from these events and assume the role of a mere observer.

When adopting the role of an observer and detaching oneself from the situation at hand, one effectively disconnects from the associated emotions.

Hence, in order to manage adverse emotions effectively, it is essential to acquire the skill of inducing a state of dissociation wherein dissociated imagery is generated rather than associated imagery. By assuming an external perspective and adopting the role of an observer, one is able to detach oneself completely from the influence exerted by the situation.

Practical task 1

Recall an event from your past. Furthermore, in the event that this occurrence remains impartial and devoid of intense emotional reactions, it can be considered most favorable. Envision the multitude of visual, auditory, and kinesthetic stimuli that you subsequently apprehended. Envision yourself within the context of this image. Consider all the visual representations sourced internally as an active participant in the ongoing proceedings.

Now envision a sense of detachment where you transcend your own self and transcend the confines of the image. You find yourself in the audience. The present image has materialized on the screen, encompassing your presence within it. You have also envisioned yourself in that situation. However, at present it merely remains as a visual representation. You are seated in the hall, observing your reflection on the monitor. Experience a sense of reliable isolation from the occurrences happening on the screen due to the discernible distance in between.

Take note of the transformation your emotions have undergone when juxtaposed with your initial response within the visual representation. The perspective from an exterior vantage point often diverges significantly from that experienced internally.

You have now acquired the experience of entering a state of dissociation and subsequently transforming the corresponding image into a dissociated representation.

You have acquired the ability to modify visual, auditory, and kinesthetic stimuli, and have successfully attained proficiency in the technique of dissociation. Therefore, you now possess a formidable instrument that enables you to alter the perception of preceding adverse encounters.

Should you still perceive a past event as exceptionally severe and incapable of resulting in anything but distress, you have the ability to effectively disengage and modify sensory signals pertaining to sight, sound, and physical sensation. You will observe a noticeable alteration in your perception, your emotional state, and your conceptualization of the past. It is already widely acknowledged that the signals entering the brain take precedence over emotions and beliefs. Emotions are initially engendered by these signals, subsequently leading to the formation of beliefs. The automatic alteration of signals invariably results in a shift in one's emotional and conceptual perspectives concerning the entirety of the event.

It is possible that you may experience astonishment when eventually perceiving the event, which initially appeared unfavorable, from a distinct perspective. The primary aspect lies in the fact that it will no longer hold significant importance for you. Rest assured, it is improbable that you will fail to recall it; your recollection will remain intact without discrepancy. However, this will merely constitute one installment within a collection of occurrences that comprise the essence of existence. Everything happens in life. Each of us must contend with challenging circumstances. However, it would be erroneous to permit a singular instance to dictate the trajectory of our entire future existence, to cast a shadow over the inherent goodness within it, and to potentially deny us promising prospects.

One may engage in daily training sessions in order to modify the perception of previous occurrences, thereby dissociating and altering the sensory stimuli reaching the brain. Commence with events of lesser significance that do not elicit intense emotions - with minor difficulties. Over time, you will acquire the ability to alter your perspective on intricate situations from the past.

Practical task 2

Indulge in a contemplative state, and subsequently recollect any form of adversity from your personal history - be it recent or remote.

Envision yourself in that predicament once more. Take note of the visual, auditory, and sensory perceptions. Could you kindly provide your perception on whether the image of this situation is linked or unlinked? In the event that the image is connected, proceed with the task of disassociation.

In order to accomplish this, one can engage in a mental exercise by envisioning the scenario unfolding on a theatrical stage, then transitioning from the stage to a vantage point in the auditorium, assuming a seated position. You have now assumed the role of a director. Modify the entirety of the signals - encompassing visual, auditory, and kinesthetic cues - in order to alleviate their intensity. Eradicate hues, diminish auditory disturbances, and minimize perceptibility of sensations. Subsequently, transform the scene into a projection, rendering the three-dimensional imagery into a two-dimensional format. Remove the sound altogether. Observe it with the discernment and attentiveness akin to that of viewing a monochromatic silent film. Subsequently, diminish the dimensions of the display. Gradually decrease the zoom level until the image becomes nearly imperceptible. Subsequently envision that the screen becomes devoid of any visual content. This motion picture has concluded, and its impact on you has ceased.

Take note of how your perspective on the situation has shifted.

Nlp Techniques: Rapport

The initial phase of NLP primarily centered around enhancing efficacy and efficiency in achieving superior outcomes within a therapeutic framework. This fundamentally revolves around the process of altering individuals' perspectives and beliefs within the context of therapy. Since this 1st wave, NLP techniques have expanded to include more fields.

During the initial stages of NLP development, the developers observed that specific behaviors and inquiries have a detrimental impact on rapport. This serves to undermine both the profoundness and the caliber of outcomes.

How people build rapport

In order to overcome this obstacle, it is necessary to establish a harmonious connection. This fundamentally pertains to imbuing a sense of proximity, ease, and familiarity among others. As you cultivate these emotions, it is imperative to uphold a sense of propriety, both in terms of adhering to societal norms and fostering personal boundaries, alongside maintaining a professional or business association.

Individuals establish rapport through various means. An alternate approach involves the act of replicating, or mirroring, as a means to achieve the desired outcome. In the realm of interpersonal communication, individuals tend to reflexively emulate the gestures, tempo, voice quality, breathing, and other behavioral cues exhibited by their counterparts. Through the implementation and integration of this methodology into the field of NLP, individuals can effectively establish and perpetuate a profound connection to facilitate enhanced communication.

Mirroring

The technique of establishing rapport through the utilization of matching and direct mirroring is considered to be a highly prevalent and efficacious approach. This method is widely employed by sales professionals and business owners to facilitate negotiations. Nevertheless, in the event that the individual in question possesses knowledge of your mirroring tactics, this approach becomes ineffectual. Occasionally, individuals display reduced levels of receptiveness and communication skills upon realizing that their counterpart is mimicking their behavior.

ALTERNATIVE METHODS FOR ESTABLISHING A CONNECTION

Fostering rapport involves cultivating a positive and mutually beneficial relationship with the individual you are engaging in a conversation with. Presented here are a compilation of the most efficacious NLP methodologies, which can be implemented to enhance one's prowess in effective communication.

Listening

An individual who possesses the ability to actively listen is adept at communicating effectively. By actively engaging in attentive listening, one demonstrates genuine curiosity in the perspectives and experiences of the interlocutor. It is important to consider that an individual possesses a singular oral opening, yet possesses a pair of auditory organs. This implies that you have the opportunity to engage in double the amount of listening compared to speaking. By actively engaging in attentive listening, one can discern the areas that necessitate additional elaboration, identify the information that the interlocutor requires additional insight on, and determine the elements that are extraneous and should be omitted, thereby enhancing the overall efficacy of the conversation.

The Other Shoe

Empathize with the perspective of the other individual. Temporarily immerse oneself in the perspective of the other individual. Determine the origin or background of this individual. Immerse yourself in the perspective of others, while insulating yourself from any detrimental influences originating from their worldview. Utilize this opportunity to enhance your receptiveness in listening. That entails solely engaging in the act of listening. The majority of individuals engage in partial listening due to being preoccupied with mentally rehearsing or preparing their forthcoming responses. NLP encourages the acquisition of the ability to acknowledge and honor the alternative perception of reality held by others.

Empathize

It is highly advantageous to demonstrate empathy rather than sympathy. Empathy entails comprehending and sharing the challenges experienced by others, while refraining from interference unless explicitly invited to do so. Expressing sympathy entails experiencing regret or sorrow on behalf of the individual in question. This phenomenon engenders a heightened sense of negativity as it is widely interpreted by the majority as a manifestation of disrespect. Expressing empathy frequently puts the other individual on the defensive. It conveys the notion that the sympathizer harbors the belief that the individual in question lacks the ability or means to independently overcome or address their own predicament.

Positive perception

Direct your attention towards the positive aspects of the individual rather than dwelling on their shortcomings. Please bear in mind that locating positive aspects can be challenging if the other individual displays difficult behavior. Moreover, the majority of individuals tend to find it more convenient, and almost innate, to perceive the downsides. It is imperative to maintain a steadfast focus on the positive aspects rather than fixating on the flaws. This viewpoint assists in fostering increased reverence in the individual. Your level of respect will be evident in both your verbal and non-verbal communication. Upon perceiving this, the intended recipient of your message will be more receptive, thereby enhancing the effectiveness of your communication.

The counterperspective

While you may possess an undeniable fervor, unwavering conviction, or profound assurance regarding your own perspectives, it is imperative to acknowledge that the opposing individual might harbor an equal amount of ardor for their own viewpoint. The divergent perspectives can pose a significant obstacle in facilitating effective communication. To overcome this obstacle, endeavor to perceive and comprehend the perspective of the other individual. Gain a perspective of the world through the lens of the other individual. Among all the methodologies available, this particular approach stands out as the foremost impactful and essential proficiency when it comes to engaging with individuals. This entails the utilization of the Perceptual Position as an established technique within the field of Neuro-Linguistic Programming (NLP). It begins with the act of empathizing and adopting the perspective of another individual. Given your current standpoint, consider the emotions you would experience. What is the perspective of the situation when viewed from that vantage point? What potential virtues could you cultivate within the context of such a circumstance? What sort of convictions could have originated from that standpoint? What potential expectations, concerns, or needs might arise?

Valuing and acknowledging the perspectives of others

Acknowledge that your perspective is not the solitary one that holds merit. Individuals form their own perspectives, which can frequently diverge from or starkly differ from one's own, as they often derive them from personal encounters or observations. Individuals undergo diverse experiences due to their unique perceptions and interpretations of their surroundings. As an illustration, if a collective of individuals were to undergo an identical occurrence, yet derive disparate interpretations from the experience. They hold distinct viewpoints and exhibit disparate reactions. Therefore, there is no uniform/consistent encounter. Additionally, it is important to acknowledge that there is no definitive or incorrect perspective on the world. It is subjective in nature, and these perspectives evolve over the course of time. Devote sufficient time to acquaint oneself with the perspectives of others. It has the potential to enhance your knowledge and foster personal growth by facilitating insights.

Take responsibility

Despite having the most favorable intentions, optimal outcomes are not always guaranteed. Regardless of the consequences or outcomes of communication, it is imperative to be fully accountable. Merely possessing good intentions is often insufficient, as individuals tend to respond primarily to the content and manner of one's communication. They lack the ability to perceive your thoughts and discern your genuine concern for their well-being. Do not anticipate them to possess the ability to perceive your true intentions and acknowledge that you have good intentions. You are entrusted with the obligation to ensure their understanding. It is imperative to maintain awareness of the impression your message conveys, as discerned from the reactions exhibited by the recipient. If their response deviates from your desired outcome and is met with a negative disposition, then consider adjusting your communication approach. Please refrain from persisting with the utilization of a communication pattern that is proving to be unsuccessful.

Acknowledge that engaging in interpersonal communication bears resemblance to navigating a complex and precarious terrain, fraught with potential hazards. Proceeding without careful consideration and presenting your spiel hastily is expected to yield unfavorable outcomes, despite possessing genuine intentions. Devise a strategy to navigate around mines or areas that evoke sensitivity, vehement opposition, or defensive responses from the other individual. Exercise caution and adapt continually. The message must be adapted to align with the cognitive disposition and current emotional state of the interlocutor during the act of communication.

Rapport with the self

To cultivate effective interpersonal connections, it is essential to foster a positive and harmonious self-relationship. Nurturing a positive demeanor towards oneself constitutes an additional measure in enhancing one's communication abilities. It is additionally an essential measure in acquiring increased self-assurance and enhanced self-worth. Having a positive demeanor towards oneself serves as a solid basis for fostering healthy interpersonal relationships.

Accept imperfections

Certain individuals aspire towards perfection, a mindset that can be deemed commendable when pursuing achievement. Nevertheless, refrain from being excessively critical of yourself should you encounter difficulties in attaining perfection. Recognize that all individuals, yourself included, possess inherent flaws. Embrace and acknowledge your vulnerabilities, imperfections, and weaknesses. These perceived "weaknesses" have the potential to be transformed into sources of strength. These attributes encompass the essence of human nature. This perspective confers a substantial drawback in the area of communication, as individuals may be less inclined to concur with your standpoint due to the inherent imperfection existing in the world. Furthermore, your imperfections serve to enhance your relatability. Collective encounters, vulnerabilities, challenges, and so forth. Serves as an excellent foundation for fostering strong relationships and enhancing communication proficiency.

"Do not overly prioritize self-importance.

Possess a good-natured and lighthearted disposition. This fosters a sense of comfort and relaxation in the presence of individuals. Additionally, it bestows upon you a charismatic disposition that attracts individuals to your presence. Cultivate the ability to humorously acknowledge your own shortcomings and graciously invite others to share in the laughter. It alleviates tension and fosters a relatable and enjoyable perception of oneself in the eyes of others.

www.ingramcontent.com/pod-product-compliance
Lightning Source LLC
Chambersburg PA
CBHW050241120526
44590CB00016B/2176